MOVE IN SILENCE

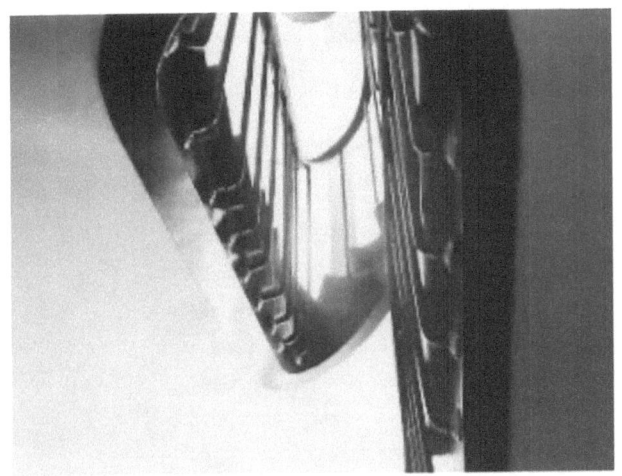

Poems by Blake Edward Hamilton

Luchador Press
Big Tuna, TX

Copyright © Blake Edward Hamilton, 2021
First Edition: 1 3 5 7 9 10 8 6 4 2
ISBN: 978-1-952411-48-9
LCCN: 2021931218

Cover art and author photo: Blake Edward Hamilton
All rights reserved. No part of this publication may be
reproduced or transmitted in any form or by any means,
electronic or mechanical, including photocopying,
recording or by info retrieval system, without prior
written permission from the author.

I am very grateful to Luchador Press for opening its arms to my work and publishing my first book with such kindness and receptivity to the process. Seldom does the act of writing take place in a vacuum. Because of this, I also want to thank the many friends, family, and colleagues who took a minute out of their busy lives to support me as a writer, which includes reading what I've written and giving crucial, honest feedback, or just listening when I needed an ear. Finishing this collection half-in and half-out of quarantine during the pandemic of 2020 has presented its own horrific and bizarre challenges; therefore, I have unlimited gratitude to the world of poets, writers, and artists in which I have been lucky enough to engage and from which I've grown as an author. With that being said, I've discovered how to keep what serves me. It's been a lengthy process, but I've learned to let go of the rest.

— B.E.H

"The Animal" was published with *Punch Drunk Press.*

TABLE OF CONTENTS

Part I: The Boat

The People From Purcell / 1

Grand Inventions / 3

Auto / Nomos / 5

Hung / 7

Untitled / 8

Hybrid Charms / 9

Mountain Road / 11

Summer, 1986 / 12

A Night Where Nothing Happens / 13

Pillows For Sale / 14

The Flood In April / 16

Hungry Neighbor Drives Off In His Car / 18

Dual On The River / 19

First Catch Of The Quarantine / 21

Beneath The Diving Board / 22

Anthem / 23

The Sociopath Kingdom / 24

The Boat / 27

Part II: Maelstrom

Doubtful Forms / 31
Plans For A Garden In Which People
   Become Lost / 33
In Silence / 39
The Animal / 40
I Got Out Of The Car Anyway / 42
Mother Despot / 52
Gaslight / 54
Death Roll / 57
Elsewhere / 59
Earhart / 60

For Tom Waits, Thom Yorke, & Till Brönner

PART I:

THE BOAT

The shore seemed refined, far away, unreal. Already the little distance they had sailed had put them far from it and given it the changed look, the composed look, of something receding in which one no longer has any part. Which was their house? She could not see it.

— To the Lighthouse, Virginia Woolf

THE PEOPLE FROM PURCELL

Lemon skin,
dancing membrane,

a yellow spark, flashing
in glass

on the old table
marked by other glasses,

half-moons where wet
soaked into the scuffs

Cs

chained to the table's edge,
hoofmarks, regular devil feet

In from the small towns,
pink pilgrim, bundle-face

false grin, cheap hair,
bodies bulging, crammed

into hamper-clothes, Trump
faces, flat-line mouths

beaten into skin, smears,
histories ground into hard living,

candy corn pumpkins year round,
and gas station holidays

beach shirts on a landlocked
Saturday —

hick accents and a raven cackle,
voices laced unconscious

Church, talking about church, talking
about their "white church,"

a raven ruptures a vocal cord; the pink
in her shirt is the soft ashes of dried Pepto.

GRAND INVENTIONS

Our best porn is social,

is media

refined exposure, public acts
triumphant; so much

sucking everyone

sucking

dopamine fuck-train
in the park

whole families,
the kids too

emojis shitting
falling, little 'like-

thumbs' falling down shirt fronts
leaky dick sluice

pouring, Look, just LIKE my post
just *like* me like it, like my

post my limbs
suck me suck my lies

whole families
everyone!

AUTO / NOMOS

If I flee at all
it's because I still believe

in self-protection —
this is when I demand

a form, place that responds;
what's left is mine.

The earth is a tether holding
our remains, and they

collapse, shattering from hard
sirens; the cliffs jutting are not

your homes, but the ship
I sail cuts against stars,

built from attempts at theft,
old comrades slipping in a finger,

and hollows dug by escaping
the others, their wet promises,

splintered feet and lassoed limbs hung
around bowed necks,

these blind spiders, rushing, tumbling
out of meaty voids,

Your form — it is a conglomeration.

Your form is patchwork sinew

Your form cannot hold

Your form cannot hold

Your form cannot hold

HUNG

In the mountains people stare,
gawking beneath brave antlers
cracking space, shadow slice
down stucco walls, down old
pits, fires disassemble across
tiles flattened hard by broken feet —
What are they seeking? What do
they seek? Am I weary, answers
somewhere on my face; they eat
the air with eyes starved and burned
hollow.
I've got love on my left, ass like
a sculpture, carved holy in blue slacks,
brown mountain boots, smooth back,
yellow stripes, yellow hat — Is there
a bathroom somewhere? Is there
somewhere we could go? Break
an antler off the wall. Slide it
into my mouth.

I gift myself little bits of timeline, an animal
digging pits in a deserted forest so it can hide
itself from marauders, the stalking herds,
grizzlies, elegant deer, bulls,

and their horns, looking for me in pockets of
jellyfish-dark, silence unheard of by the seekers.

HYBRID CHARMS

Your fingers give
you away

feathers catch sun,
slick purple glint

look, you wipe them
clean of sound

You rescue others,
and bury your colors

and bleed your wings,
methodical, trenchant waste,

wide-pupil-dive, save us
both this time

from your quiet, your reticence
your refusal,

to let a touch linger,
to dissolve suggestion

You run off — stars over
our heads —

and leave the furniture
outside, for escaped dogs

to sniff and lick, to piss,
and make homes

for themselves until
the sun breaks on them,

and the ground is wet

MOUNTAIN ROAD

Nightmare resting place, a proper burial, peaks
saluting spectacular tortures, tunnels broken,
saturated, quick floods, bonds built in humiliation.

Sprig of nightshade; Spring spreads her legs, egg
sacks, pools of coagulant, poisonous buds, lifting,
her holes remain ready; viper homes, arachnid paradises.

Distance. Antidote. Escape. A willing meal. Lie down
and open. Web-tongue, eight-legged throat; parasite twitch,
third eye dermis — a body for a body, minerals in the blood.

Sunset spill, magenta, dead desert town, dust roads, boarded
diner, humming truck, blue near an orange horizon, a slit, a bony
eagle descending at the shudder. Snatch of furry muscle, newborn.

Beak-twist, neck-snap, the rustle of fields in the empty.

SUMMER, 1986

fish tank on the desk, newt corpse
staring, proud chest, the maid vacuuming

carefully negotiating territory, gray carpet,
Star Wars toys piled desperate

at night i have a hallway

I carve names into it with my pocketknife,
my passage to the castle

butter on the stairs, we slide
doors open, baked-brick-feet,

sap leak, and the ribbon tied around
the wooden post, tree fort swings

through the windows: *Beverly Hills Cop* on HBO
Dad and the couch alone, with a beer, staring

crickets shake the air,
a lawnmower three yards away, chopping.

A NIGHT WHERE NOTHING HAPPENS

Wind gust, the edge of the sunken room.
chimes in the eaves, metal click bathed cold.

The room with the bed, nothing moves.

Stars burst on the lake, freeze, water stunned,
a stray light, sourceless, lands on the rocks.

Ducks huddle, shudder, wings lifting,
the moon, a raw coin adrift, clouds swimming

near the towers, windowless, and the highway
blocked.

Trees wall-in the homes, the cul-de-sac.

Headlights, ghost eyes, puncture the dark,
and drive away.

Traffic on the road rustles; the wind
consumes it.

PILLOWS FOR SALE

Rain only sounds like itself
in a locked car. Wind shoves
dead cacti. Parking lot frozen.
World baptized in silence. No
one will attack you; they just
keep walking. Who is the strange
guy sitting in his car? I don't know;
keep walking.

The rain says, "It's too late."
Says, "Here, you can't be touched."

Hermetic bliss is rooted in a vacuum
sealed automobile, parked at the door
of a shop that sells pillows.

The store is empty — the clerk's
face is despair through the window,
through the signs, a despair
that echos, that holds.

The people don't move or notice
the headlights across the glass,
the thunder, the water pouring down
the walls.

The sun is the only thing.

                         Cold dies in its shadow.
                         Warmth heals contractions

laid like thorns across bare roads.

                         Winter is romanticized; it's
                         something ugly we have to fuck,

to wake up to, struggling breath.

                         A wet cough on your lips, no

apology;

                         it leaves residuals of itself
                         around the house;

it doesn't wipe;

                         It doesn't flush; but
                          it eats everything

even bone

THE FLOOD IN APRIL

Thunder boulder dropped
chasmal, world slashed wet,
parking lot pond, trees
sprung, verdient explosions
under a gray moat.

You can locate yourself
in cataclysm; let it collapse.

Walls include their own
disintegration. It's embedded
in their seams. People imitate
people until death, and it's
embedded.

From the gray, flashes of white,
distortions through fog, slipping
across old throats and children,
neglected, playing with a ball
in a driveway alone, soaked.

The grocery store, a woman wears
a mask, and sweats, picking up
lemons. People stare and run. They
are sick with a virus they will later
spread, eating chicken fingers in
a chain restaurant.

The woman goes home, sees no one. At 80, they have all died; she does not remember them. Her garden floods. She still sees no one.

HUNGRY NEIGHBOR DRIVES OFF IN HIS CAR

Protoplasm sky, fire of clouds, bleach in the wasp nest,
corrupting eggs. Desert pinecone, sideways slant, water
dried brittle, and hidden in breaths of shadow

by the parking garage, empty concrete, patchwork skin,
weed-ridden, boner-red fire hydrant, bursting proud
at the corner

Poor lonely neighbor, hair parted thick, parted, gentle
face, heavy wounded mouth yelling, frantic tumble,
he breaks things, and I hear him

beat off

on the other side, our shared wall, slow mechanics,
piston lurch of his boney hips; I wonder, does he
want his cum to shatter through, to leap the boundary?

Helmet pushing against thin shorts, and bird legs, white,
sprinkles of red-brown hair, red-brown, those slashes,
parking lot skin, ass-crack-oxygen-mask, you'd breathe

with a mouthful, video game thumbs, a daughter somewhere,
carseat in the back of the car seat, fading pale, too much time
in the sun, between the dumb drop of your sack, between

inner thigh, yellow socks left, sour feet, clammy sloth
arms, lowering, you spread wide, split open, arms and legs
folding, this is how much you want it

DUAL ON THE RIVER

*I check my mail, latex gloves (the FED EX man is getting a blowjob,
ass moving in one of the windows),*

*quarantine street, a bike on its side, wheels spin, overcast echo,
a hammer lifting and hitting spanish tile.*

On a mound, flagrant green, creek stench, abandoned of bodies,
of sound,
the river meets its ends, cuts silver around moss banks and cold
stones

around coiled swan bodies and ducks stacking themselves (in
Nature, it has
to be *forced* to get it done), and the tearing apart, darting, water
catching sun

and breaking across itself, shuddering away, container for other
mute bodies,
silent injustices, and then two shadows spilling from themselves,
liquid

repeated, bending over green, a body tilt, a jounce forward, a
motion meant to filet.

The couple wears N95 masks. In a place bereft of people, they
  loom, hunch
like commas, soft ribs, and lean into each other,

each clutching a thin sword, each angling for a strike at the
  other, and on tip-toes
bounce across the river's bank, fencing in a vacuum

by way of biological holocaust; man, however, continues himself.
Here, swords meet, sharp circles; here, a dual witnessed by
  no one.

FIRST CATCH OF THE QUARANTINE

The crab is the blue of the gods,
unmatched, a body sectioned, pincer
stretching, pincer wide, half-face,
half-eye, diagonal dissection,

three legs, arachnid ballet, spreading blue
biceps connecting a ribbed forearm,
pincer snapped, underbelly grid,

and the fork at an angle
nestling the crest of butter,

the white plate,

and beyond this

famished children scream
at the tide,

at the bucket
of blue bodies.

BENEATH THE DIVING BOARD

Burn me through, cool touch of air on my face,
smoke smell, ocean blue from still water

where torsos dissolve

The row houses, emptied.
The glass, changed.

Who knew what these windows saw;
how they prevented us from counting
cavernous rooms, people examining

miniature beds, armoires, thumb-
sized chairs, forks like a splinter

held / cradled in indigenous palms.

*in, inward, inside, interfere
injure, integrate, instill*

inch past me — with your magic body,
here, the pool is a mausoleum, gossamer

tile, liquid-blue diamond-water, up to your arms, swim,
a god gave you the tide, tilt — your head, lean into

the cloud stratum, you're a mistake, your posture is all wrong,
you leap, and the glass shatters the water to sound.

ANTHEM

you've come this far, you've come forward
you've come across old mountains, barehanded,
no one to help you survive,

silences attached to you,
held you to port, you've been gored, whipped,
knotted, bound to fences, your friends have
left you, and yet, you went on, you have a body
made up of maps, hope (that you could continue),

has been cut out of you,
what you grew of your own is webbed wire,
a few of your friends have tried to kill you
with their deaths, and you had to let them
down. Not everyone has what you have.

THE SOCIOPATH KINGDOM

Communicate honesty to a row of pigs
eating their own shit.

Tell them, Hey, there is a moral compass;
make it sound important,

make it sound critical, give it a voice.
Our examination of 'right' and 'wrong'

begins at a pig's rectum, somewhere in there,
a thick wad of cash.

Pigs have no sense of direction; if they did,
it would go unheeded.

Better to wander aimless, towers and halls,
roadways through trough chum, fecal museums,

streets disemboweled, a rain of variety meats,
on the cobblestones. Humanity is this

wandering, compass crushed long ago.
Rather, auto-fellatio shines in all hearts,

a 24 hour suck job, and the people will
tell you, mid-suck, how good they

are with their tongues, like pigs, troughs
overturned, waddling in gastric timeshares.

In this Kingdom, your sucking talents
can save you from the grill,

second only to the tongue action, little
piggy tail flick, a fly

nestles in the grease, but here, *here*, the pigs
rule; consciousness is forfeit, compassion

is a pruning knife wedged in a windpipe,
searching. Pigs don't eat compassion, but
a strict calorie count of one-upmanship,

the Kingdom demands the rich output
of self-comparison, of ghosting, iced

shrugs. The false smile is the path to God
in the mid-town *Jamboree!* Survival

here is contingent on the amount
of make-up videos you have on YouTube

produced by major publications. *Look
how she does it! Oh my!* Our Kingdom is not

bankrupt, just ask the pigs; they have
the best smiles; make-up routines,

incomparable. Paint your face in shit,
so you can go to the party; the Kingdom

only invites the best — everyone else
has streaming. We're told morality

is the true source of constipation;
you can't suffocate your neighbors

and their pets, slowly, if you haven't shit
for days. And everyone in this tower beams

from the sound of their own hands, the swinging
chops, the rustles their bodies make

as they climb over — on top of — piles
of themselves — the prize awaits!

They reach, they lunge, there's blood.

The pigs, they nestle. The stars overhead
are bright.

THE BOAT

Out there, a boat is sinking; it's just a dash
of blue-black against red, a figure,

and then the horizon. The ocean is coal,
and the sky bulges in soot-bellies, rain ready

to burst. Static-crackle, lightening pulse,
a flutter of wind and ocean ripples

up to the piers where the people stand
and watch the boat sink, hands holding hats

firm to vague heads, so they won't blow
away. A yellow-orange flame licks out

from the center of the boat, its masts taut
in its struggle to stay up, even as it's eaten

by the deep rage, the flames bursting
boards in an intersection of its gut, little slashes

of men racing around, and then, a crooked
lowering of lifeboats, sagging on thin ropes;

the ship tilts proud, bowsprit up to the drowning
sun, washed bright, splintered shadow at the rim

of clouds moving over, and across, and someone
calls out, a sound like wind and glass breaking,

someone says, *Do something!* and the hull
bursts again, the ship fragmenting into two

separate pieces, one still proud, the other languishing,
drifting, sinking further, bound in opaque smoke,

water like slate, like a mouth, and then the fins
come, little sharp triangles forming at a distance,

tentacles reach from black waves, liquid glint,
waiting until the storm begins.

PART II:
MAELSTROM

... it is a general law of nature, that bids all to eat, and to be eaten in their turn...

— G.T. Black, *The Principles of the Natural Laws of Man*, Etc, 1837

DOUBTFUL FORMS

all human matter is constructed
of hidden intentions

> every push to get to the front of the line
> every digital social media exhalation

you have to be psychic to survive
you have to read matter

> smiles blind like UV rays
> little shards from the sky

containers of expression are like leeches
continuance is built-in

> systematic, the form fights to get here
> it crawls, placenta sac tunnel

a feast for microorganisms, virus parades
how doubtful it is for even the smallest

> later, when it's grown, it will claim Greatness
> vaccinated with gratitude for the self

the form makes more of itself,
it can't help it

        on social media, pictures will be shown
        no one gets to see the cave, though, the tracks

it happened out of thin air
the forms are magic, they say

        some wilt and perish, and some are not found
        later they will be dug up, put into museums

similar forms will come, they will stand and stare
at the bone statue in the glass case

        plaques tell them the significance, the meaning
        these forms always require meaning

PLANS FOR A GARDEN IN WHICH PEOPLE BECOME LOST

(Why was the garden abandoned in the first place? The woman shivering in the frock coat.)

I. BRAMBLES

Her clit, was all she could think, a white stocking snatched
thorny curvature of seed droppings, nodes of tiny erections

They cling, she says, *the damn things cling*. Walking, walking now,
the path directs them, lavender umbrella straight, pointing

The woman she took tea with stays back an inch. Maybe she's
afraid of the umbrella, the way she swings it, left then right.

The sting of these damn things. Oh I know, was all she could say,
heading forward, heading away from the shrubs and the green

everywhere; there's green everywhere, and it's getting on her,
she can feel it, wet, some tiny leak, something ripped near

her ankle, and she's sure it's bleeding, now. *Should I ask the*
   woman:
Please peer down, I believe I may have opened something?

She wants to dig in, hands soft in gloves that don't do much,
but she wants to dig, and they're almost there, around the
   corner,

and she can't remember how they started, how she began, or even where the woman went, because it's late now, and the
   umbrella

got left behind.

II. BERRY JUICE

It was a simple task. The edge of the fountain, derelict space, people
seldom stood there. It becomes commandeered by dead vines, leaves.

To sneak something, the laws have to provide a place to hide, or
it won't work. The pleasure is in the hiding, the cover up, not

the act itself, which demands rain, clouds like a burned wall, skin
open, bared, the clothes are meant to be removed anyway;
their design is a mechanism; take them off, put them on, reveal
a handful, handfuls are possible, heaps of thin blue flesh, orbs

purple in spots, laced green, coiled twigs, brittle umbilicus
that once held an origin somewhere, where this started

pressure, so little, and color finds its way in, paints quiet
gullets, hearts, and the wind splashes fountain water, trees

groan, the sky opens and

III. NATURE

getdownandsuckitthat'srightsuckitsuckmycockyoufuckintrollopebitch

do et quick like, while no bodies lookin' ats right, the ole thing, now ets got tu be fahster, the ole thing, the ole thing, ats right

oo if ya dun't ave a tongue on yous, if ya dun't ave a tongue!

ee ya fuckin' bitch, ya suck me, ya take it all,

quick now, nah bodies ere, hurray! Och damn, ya damn teeth!

ets a nice edge here, nice tree, nobody lookin' oh now ere it comes

take it, take it, take it, take it, take it, take it, take it, take it,

Och damn, now move, move, undue your flaps ere, undue the strings,

get it out now, the snake, I'll take to my knee, take to my knee, I'll take it

IV. THE MAZE

Hoof stamp. The promise of an exit. Sound whittled. Hedge walls
just doing their job, keeping everyone in, the outside out

Something's been here, she swears, she's sure of it, she's come this
way already, and it's a long way, back around the same corner,

back around the last, the turn that goes a bit deeper, but leads
 narrow,
a trick, and the mist doesn't help, it gathers over the green, over
the edge of the walls, covers doorways, passages, she wants a
 passage,
this is one long path, another hoof stamp, another beat of feet
 behind

her, up in the sky, it's unclear if it's a moon or a sun, but the stars
aren't there, so maybe that's a clue, but her white leather booties

split apart; there was a rock, who tosses a rock over the wall,
 condemning it
here, the path, otherwise, is clear, a dirt lane stamped into
 packed earth,

another turn, here, another edge, this corner, here, the same
 sundial
cement pillar, vines strangling it, wooden hands knotted,
 a shoe

on its side, just laying there, just left, whose is it, who leaves a
 single

shoe, tossed aside like that, laces squiggling around in the mud, flaps

limp, a dead thing; should I take it, she wonders, in case I pass
her, she may still be in here, the woman, should I look, how would

I know her, surely she'd be limping, barefoot, a torn stocking, should I?
I may not be around this corner again, but of course, I might, I passed

it once, but she wasn't sure, really, if she had

IN SILENCE

incantation

ritual

intention

———————

This is how you save yourself:

if you speak (about it), if you speak (to others), about
   your movements,
they will take you *from* them — them from you

Speak (nothing), Give (no sound), Move (in the dark)

your gift is to withhold your stories

your nature is to tell them

your sanctum is divided

People take.

THE ANIMAL

The animal
doesn't
know
why
it's been nuzzled
carried, groped, brushed
or its "purpose"
in the delicate cage
it could easily break
and it doesn't own a concept
for freedom
it doesn't see
the stretch of land
beyond the wires
as a possibility
for a homestead
off the grid
or a retreat
it doesn't retreat
or a set of dunes
for off-roading
itself into liberty
or a safe venue
for the bourgeois
emotional transcendence
that can only take place
at a concert - it hasn't

found spiritual freedom
it has a corner
that it shits in
and a trough right next to it
and it goes where the others go
and still gets nuzzles
before its hung up head down
and split top to bottom
happy-jostle of innards spilling
like a delicate swirl
on a freedom pastry,
strawberry-pink, and bright

I GOT OUT OF THE CAR ANYWAY

1.

Every man I've ever loved
Was straight.

We all were once
Forced into it

At recess, by mom and dad,
The curious neighbors.

One of them is married
And lives in Florida

With a bunch of dogs
And a husband 30 years

Older than him. He speaks
To me once before we stop

Speaking altogether,
And we know

There's nothing
Left to say.

He tells me, "Straight people are fascinating."

He says this
Like they are blind

Yet can still make a mean
Pasta dish without spilling

Anything in the kitchen,
lights off.

My relationships once
Had parameters.

No one felt entitled
To anything.

This was before Bush
And the Twin Towers collapsed.

I almost married a woman,
Who now smashes protons in Sweden.

She writes to me
On my 35th birthday.

An apology,
For using my father's

Death as an opportunity
To harm me "emotionally."

Twenty years after we break
Up, like a gang hit, she says,

This is for you being gay.

But if I want to have a 'dialog'
With her, she is open to that.

2.

When I am pistol-whipped
And mugged

The sidewalk splits into fours
— Inter-dimensional space —

Right there, immediate,
And my orange blood

Is reaffirming and bright
On all its levels.

> A friend holds me
> So I can stand
> In front of the pale cop
> With sociopath-blue eyes
> And a jaw like a tusk,
> Like a cop, as I answer
> His questions, but I'm shaking
> And the dumb eager bulge

In his black pants
Is all I want to look
At while I bleed and shake
And see what real death is like,
Feels like, when he asks, cold,
Gun-tongue, typewriter teeth:
"Can you describe them?"

'They wore white t-shirts,"
I tell him, ready to collapse.

But I want to tell him more.
He stops me, says,

"That's all I need to know,"
and I'm asked if I want an ambulance.

It'll cost me though — 500.00 bucks,
America has never been shy

About bartering to the needy
And vulnerable, Hell,

Sell the guy a ride!

I am lucky because my friend,
Who has a voice like a mother,

Says she'll drive me.
At the ER, the nurse

Shouts during the X-rays that
It's the Gun & Knife Show!

After 1:00 AM,
She speaks only of the gangs.

My face
Looks like the Elephant Man

I have a shelf pointing
From my temple

After the exam, the doctor
Says the scar tissue is staying.

I go to trauma therapy
Every day for three months

And the woman
Tells me to be thankful

To my attackers
To find gratitude

To appreciate, and
When I ask her why

She says because they chose
Not to shoot me

Through the back of my head.

A jogger finds my wallet
Tossed into bushes, and calls.

I can't leave or stand
For very long,

So my mother picks it up.
I no longer use a wallet.

3.

The last date I go on
Is with a surgeon

Who says his entire life
Has been shaped for him

By his mother;
He says he never wanted

To be a surgeon.
On our second date

He leaves me with his dog,
Which sits in a cage

In his room,
Not to be let out.

When he comes back,
He tells me

My uniqueness
Might be a problem,

Whatever that means.
He tells me

He's closeted,
But it's for the best

Because, he says,
It might be the twenty-first century

But where he's from…
And he implicates everything else.

4.

Chris, the guy from Florida,
Would spend hours in my car

Telling me about the women
He loved, how much

He was attracted
To them.

He laughed
When I looked at him.

I could hear his father
Speaking

And every other
Small town, American

Male, speaking, asserting,
Fighting.

All gay men fight; you just don't see it
Happen.

It happens later
When they want

More than half.
When their dads

Are finally dead.
I get asked on dates a lot,

My phone app is like a vending machine
Of rude dick.

But they're accommodating at least.

I could meet this guy in the parking
Garage paint closet

Of his apartment complex.
He says it's just pipes and dust

And buckets inside, and no one else.
He says we could shoot

The floor. He says his roommates
Are home.

Another asks me if I like nachos,
Then says we should get nachos,

Have sex, I don't know,
Something, but I hope

You're cool with my stats:
I'm only into 'masc' guys.

He says, "I'm attracted
To men who do not look or act 'gay'

I want a man who acts like a man."

I think of my attackers.
I think of gratitude.
I think of the back of my head.

5.

The cop's big-dick-bulge
Has an intention.

His cold fingers
Belong to another body.

They rasp filling out

The dry form; his ridiculous
Wedding ring is a tiny assertion.

All men want to be with other men.
They just push it down, push it away.

Or they get what they want,
Then push it down later.

I wonder if this cop ever keeps it down.

MOTHER DESPOT

Miscarriage born
from the body

of a staggering calf
dragging a mess,

a steaming pile, vein-sack,
purple-throb, mucous-trail

up the hill, up the vacant
patch, innocent bramble

witness to the steam,
the brief mistake spilling,

its cord dangling, like a broken
tongue from a chewed mouth.

Form found indistinguishable
in the pile, the mess, yet

you stood up anyway
against your better form,

the way you should have
stayed in the world.

This is what happens
when detritus demands

breath, when animal refuse
seeks worth.

Mothers don't go crazy
and leave their children

because of mystery;
they leave when they see

what they made,
and despair.

GASLIGHT

1.

The thing about History
is everyone gets a chance.

Daughters are sold by fathers:
Human trafficking

is always popular; ingenuity
was never a human strong suit.

Can finally buy a blu-ray
player, can finally throw a party.

2.

Modernity: the story about mothers,

and their children; rough ground, urban sites
pitted in scarfed, wet street positions;

infants cradled cold, begging.
The children often died.

But mothers had more, tirelessly, crammed
into red brick tenement houses;

slick wallpaper tongues, sagging ceiling
bowls, brown blooms, bodies on bone,

old fires, rot-exhalation, skin flakes,
mauve rash, sweat-lips, hangnail tug –

impulse fuck in the corner, indignant cum
trying so hard

to reach an egg.

3.

A cough from the mattress, snoring, worn
Dickens under a mutilated candle, a mug,
a whisky puddle. Cobblestone streets

and progress: In Whitechapel, a man rips
his way into Romanticism, and no one's going
to tell him no.

4.

The desert has a penchant for upping the odds.
Mothers explain that the Creator has never feared

sand traps; Bob and Mitch need somewhere
to go after work when Pappy is no longer alive

to toss balls in the front yard, like good men
(gee golly); all of that seed dropped

into the ground right at their feet; sip and belch,
Bob warns Mitch with throaty confidence

that he's having a daughter. Men are so proud
of his sack of clubs, the quiet spume behind his golf

cart on the way to the last hole, pinned with a tiny
red flag.

DEATH ROLL

When I look at the world, I see people who don't know who
   they are.
I see emulators. I see pick-pockets. I see bone pickers.

In America, if you move enough, you discover there aren't a lot
   of places to move.

Rather,

there are versions of places with the same people emulating
   other people
until they find a person they want to pick-pocket,

stealing faces from other faces, and then slipping them on for
   others who
do the same thing. Underneath, no telling what's there.

This has become survival.

Oh so that's who *you* are.

In most places, showing too much skin can get you killed.
In Australia, crocodiles crush their victims between their jaws,

and then pull them under and roll and roll and roll until its dead,
and then they stuff the prize into a corner, and wait until later

to eat it.

This way, the crocodile survives to make more of itself. In the future,
its children will do the same.

ELSEWHERE

Please pass me the plate on the far end of the plaid
blanket. Watch the grass, I just bought this at West Elm.

Please, I want the last hunk of Swiss and the summer sausage.

       Greasy and tight with its rectal cap.

Help me! Mmm, the sun, yes, a quick kiss, oh that's nice.

Why don't they *move* the ambulance, it's messing up everything.
I can't relax with all this death around me; it's so annoying.

Yeah, I wore one to go into Whole Foods, but, like, if you're
    gonna get it,
you're gonna get it. Like… the 1800s, Spanish Flu, duh…

We're obviously better off; much more under control.

I know, the bodies on the street are *such* an eyesore.

Oh, that's a nice breeze… I want another one and another one.

EARHART

Did you think your bones
would become a mystery;

that researchers would puzzle
over the ones they found?

Are they *you?* This is what they ask.
Everyone's busy trying to find

out where you went; they sky
shrugs, and the sand had its tongue

cut out.

Bones in question, scattered
across a beach, an island,

the sunny Pacific, your final
stop. You were everywhere,

known to aeronauts, aviator-witness,
the earth as space fragment,

a tumbling stone. Above it, you
claimed other mysteries

from the hands of dead men
and books worn to debris.

Did you think, amidst clouds
and gods and hidden cities,

that you would break records
for disappearances?

We want to traipse through
the ruins of your crash;

the way of all unanswered
mysteries, things that were.

We want to find you so
we can guess at how you

evolved into inscrutability,
into something that responds

in gestures, hints in time,
guesses. They say crabs found

you, divided you up, coconut crabs,
armored-plated, hulking tarantulas

in paradise; they say,
the giant crabs took you from

yourself; Nature up-close, rather
than from above, from a distance;

Nature takes from the sky. It eats
the gods, and in return, gives us

silence.

Blake Edward Hamilton holds an MFA in Creative Writing from Naropa University, and currently teaches college English. His work has appeared in *World Literature Today Magazine: Windmill, NPR, Bombay Gin Literary Journal, The Guerrilla Lit Mag., South Broadway Press,* and *Punch Drunk Press,* among others. He is the author of the poetry collection, *All Through Your Multiple Selves.*

www.ingramcontent.com/pod-product-compliance
Lightning Source LLC
Chambersburg PA
CBHW030350100526
44592CB00010B/894